MUMBAI
TRAVEL GUIDE
2024

Mumbai Marvels: Exploring India's Vibrant Metropolis

Philip Mablood

**Copyright 2023, Philip Mablood.
All Rights Reserved!**
No part of this book may be reproduced, stored in a retrieval system, or transmitted in any form or by any means, electronic, mechanical, photocopying, recording, or otherwise, without written permission of the copyright owner.

TABLE OF CONTENTS

Introduction
    Welcome to Mumbai
    Geographical Location of Mumbai
    Understanding Mumbai's Essence
    Best time to visit
Chapter 1: Unveiling Mumbai's History
    Historical Overview
    Architectural Heritage
    Iconic Landmarks
Chapter 2: Navigating Mumbai's Neighborhoods
    Exploring South Mumbai
    Venturing through Central Mumbai
    Embracing Suburban Mumbai
Chapter 3: Cultural Encounters
    Arts and Entertainment
    Festivals and Celebrations
    Local Traditions and Customs
Chapter 4: Culinary Delights
    Street Food Extravaganza
    Regional Cuisines
    Fine Dining Experiences
Chapter 5: Urban Exploration
    Bustling Markets and Bazaars
    Modern Skyline and Infrastructure
    Green Spaces and Retreats
Chapter 6: Day Trips and Excursions
    Nearby Getaways

- Beach Escapes
- Historical Day Trips

Chapter 7: Practical Information
- Transportation Guide
- Accommodation Options
- Essential Tips for Travelers

Chapter 8: Insider's Recommendations
- Offbeat Experiences
- Hidden Gems and Local Favorites
- Insider Tips for Exploring Mumbai

Chapter 9: Responsible Tourism
- Sustainable Travel Practices
- Supporting Local Communities
- Responsible Tourism Initiatives

Chapter 10: Conclusion
- Farewell to Mumbai
- Lasting Memories and Reflections

Introduction

Welcome to Mumbai

Welcome to Mumbai: Embracing the Heartbeat of India's Vibrant Metropolis

Mumbai, often known as the "City of Dreams," is a vibrant city that truly captures the essence of India's diversity, energy, and vitality. Tucked away on the Arabian Sea's coast, this international metropolis is a hive of activity, culture, and enticing appeal that draws visitors from all over the world.

A Tapestry of History and Modernity

Mumbai's fascinating past, once known as Bombay, is told via layers that each adds to the city's intricate and varied fabric. Mumbai has changed into a mingling pot of cultures, customs, and goals from its native Koli fishing villages to its colonial past under Portuguese and British administration.

Iconic Landmarks and Architectural Splendors

Mumbai's historic past is told through a variety of architectural wonders that may be seen as you navigate the busy streets of the city. Every building, from the majestic Taj Mahal Palace to the imposing Gateway of India, which represents the imperial past, carries stories from bygone times.

A Melting Pot of Cultures and Traditions

Mumbai's vibrant fusion of cultures, languages, and customs is what makes it so appealing. This dynamic city welcomes individuals from all backgrounds and offers a multicultural mosaic where tradition and modernity coexist peacefully. From the vibrant exuberance of Navratri to the festive celebration of Ganesh Chaturthi, the city throws celebrations with great zeal.

Culinary Odyssey: Indulge in Gastronomic Delights

Get ready for a unique and amazing culinary tour around Mumbai. Mumbai offers a feast for the senses, satisfying every palate from enjoying mouthwatering street food treats like vada pav and pav bhaji in busy local markets to savoring the true flavors of regional cuisines at upscale dining facilities.

Urban Exploration: Where Tradition Meets Innovation

Mumbai is a city that skillfully combines the allure of the past with the emerging modernity evident in its skyscrapers, vibrant markets, and entertainment districts. Discover the modern beat of the city by venturing into the bustling nightlife of Bandra or the colorful bazaars of Colaba Causeway.

Warmth and Hospitality of Mumbai

People in the city are hospitable and friendly, despite their fast-paced exterior. Visitors are made to feel at home and loved in this vibrant city by the warmth and generosity of Mumbai's people, who exhibit a spirit of resilience in the face of hardship.

The Gateway to Unforgettable Adventures

Outside the city limits, Mumbai is the starting point for a multitude of amazing experiences. Discover the neighboring Elephanta ancient caves or take a break from the bustle of the city by visiting the peaceful Alibaug beaches.

A City That Leaves a Lasting Impression

Mumbai leaves a lasting impression on every tourist, whether they are drawn in by its opulent architecture, fascinated by its cultural diversity, or enthralled by its mouthwatering cuisine. It's a city that remains in the mind, luring visitors to come back and take advantage of everything that it has to offer.

In Mumbai, each encounter makes a lasting impression on your spirit, every street has a story to tell, and every corner has a hidden gem. So go out on this adventure through the busy streets, vibrant marketplaces, and varied neighborhoods to uncover Mumbai's true nature, a city that never ceases to astound, inspire, and extend a warm welcome.

Geographical Location of Mumbai

India's western coast is home to Mumbai, formerly known as Bombay. Situated on the Arabian Sea's Konkan coast, it serves as the capital city of Maharashtra state. Mumbai's coordinates are roughly 19.0760° North latitude and 72.8777° East longitude. The city is spread out over a peninsula and is made up of seven islands that were combined to create the thriving metropolis of today by land reclamation. Because of its advantageous coastal location, it has long been an important port city, which has boosted its stature both economically and culturally in India.

Understanding Mumbai's Essence

Exploring Mumbai's complex identity, which is weaved from historical, cultural, and social strands, is essential to understanding the city's character.
1. Melting Pot of Cultures:

Mumbai's diversity is what makes it so special. It's a colorful mosaic where many languages, customs, and civilizations coexist peacefully. The city welcomes residents from all areas and origins, resulting in a diverse fabric of festivals, cultures, and ways of life.

2. Spirit of Resilience:
Mumbai has a resilient spirit. Its citizens demonstrate incredible fortitude and solidarity in the face of hardships, including floods, terrorist attacks, and social inequality. The city's fabric is woven with this tenacity.

3. Urban Contrasts:
Mumbai is an extreme juxtaposition. It displays the opulence of contemporary buildings, upscale fashion, and entertainment in addition to the unvarnished charm of the city's slums and the ease of everyday life. These contrasts draw attention to how dynamic and complicated the city is.

4. Economic Hub and Bollywood:
Mumbai, the financial center of India, is a hive of business activity. The main stock exchanges, corporate headquarters, and

entrepreneurial ventures in the nation are located there. Mumbai is also the center of Bollywood, the Indian film industry that has a global impact on entertainment and culture.

5. Fusion of Heritage and Modernity:
The core of the city is a fusion of fast modernity and historical tradition. Modern infrastructure, cutting-edge industries, and a fast-paced way of life mix with historical sites, colonial architecture, and long-standing customs.

6. The City of Dreams:
Mumbai is referred to as the "City of Dreams," a place where dreams come true. Dreams are fostered, chances abound, and people from all walks of life swarm to achieve their goals, whether they be in business, entertainment, the arts, or finance.

7. A Culinary Journey:
Mumbai is also best enjoyed for its varied food offerings. The city's gastronomy offers a delicious exploration of flavors and reflects its multiculturalism with everything from scrumptious street food to beautiful fine dining experiences.

8. Warmth and Hospitality:
Mumbai is a crowded city, yet it has a kind, welcoming vibe. Mumbaikars, the inhabitants, are renowned for being amiable and helpful, which gives guests a feeling of community.

Exploring this mixture of cultures, resiliency, contrasts, ambitions, and the special fusion of tradition and modernity is key to comprehending Mumbai's core. It's a call to discover the city's layers, each of which reveals a different aspect of its alluring character.

Best time to visit

The months of November through February are usually the finest times to visit Mumbai. Compared to the rest of the year, these months have comparatively milder and cooler weather. With temperatures between 15°C (59°F) and 30°C (86°F), it's the perfect time of year for touring, outdoor activities, and leisurely exploring the city's attractions.

The lively mood of the city is enhanced by the numerous festivals and celebrations that fall within this time frame. It's crucial to remember, though, that this is the busiest travel season, which could result in more expensive lodging and more visitors to well-known tourist destinations.

When visiting Mumbai, it may be best for visitors to avoid the monsoon season (June to September), which is known for its intense rainfall and ability to hamper outdoor activities.

The ideal time to visit Mumbai ultimately comes down to personal choices for the weather, events, and level of crowding. Travelers should organize their itinerary according to their interests and the things they hope to see while visiting this vibrant city.

Chapter 1: Unveiling Mumbai's History

Historical Overview

Here is a brief history of Mumbai, including its development from prehistoric periods to its current state as a flourishing metropolis:
Historical Overview of Mumbai: Tracing the City's Rich Heritage and Evolution
Mumbai's history is a tapestry weaved over centuries, full of trade, cultural fusion, conquests, and transformations. The city's history begins in antiquity, when it saw the rise and fall of empires, colonial rule, and finally its transformation into the thriving metropolis it is today.
Ancient Origins:
Mumbai's history is earliest known to have been written in 250 BCE when the area was populated by native Koli fishermen. The region was made up of seven different islands connected by mangroves and

creeks: Wadala, Mahim, Parel, Old Woman's Island, Colaba, and Mazagaon.

Medieval Period:

Several dynasties, notably the Gujarat Sultanate and the Silhara dynasty, ruled Mumbai in the fourteenth century. Because of their natural harbor, the islands were strategically significant. Portuguese explorers led by Vasco da Gama were drawn to the islands and landed there in 1498.

Colonial Era:

The islands were seized by the Portuguese in 1534, giving them a crucial foothold in their growing trading network. They called the region "Bombaim," which is thought to have come from the Portuguese word "Bom Bahia," which means "Good Bay." However, Bombay was given to the British East India Company in 1661 as part of a dowry deal between King Charles II of England and Portugal.

Rise of British Bombay:

During the British era, Bombay quickly developed into a major trading hub. The city's rise drew numerous communities, including Parsis, Jews, and Muslims, encouraging cultural diversity and economic prosperity. The East India Company improved the city's infrastructure, stimulated trade, and created defenses, notably the iconic "Bombay Castle."

Gateway to India:
Major structures like the Gateway of India and Victoria Terminus (now Chhatrapati Shivaji Maharaj Terminus) were built in the 19th century to represent Bombay's rise to prominence as a major port and British Raj administrative hub.

Struggle for Independence:
A center of political activism during India's independence movement, the city was established. During the 1942 Quit India Movement, which was characterized by large-scale demonstrations and acts of civil disobedience against British colonial rule, Bombay was a key player.

Post-Independence Era:
Bombay was the capital of the Bombay State after India gained independence in 1947. This continued until 1960 when Mumbai was created as the capital of the new state of Maharashtra. The city became

a bustling metropolis as a result of its quick industrialization, economic expansion, and urbanization.

Modern Mumbai:

Mumbai has developed over the past few decades into a major hub for the Bollywood film industry, a global financial hub, and a draw for immigrants looking for better prospects. Towering buildings dot the city's skyline, and its colorful blend of tradition and modernity is still reflected in its cultural fabric.

Mumbai is a living example of a city that has persevered over time, embracing both the opportunities and challenges of the twenty-first century while still honoring its rich historical heritage. Its development from a collection of islands to the commercial and entertainment hub of India is reminiscent of the country's own story of expansion, variety, and vibrancy.

Mumbai's journey from modest beginnings to its current status as a booming metropolis is captured in this historical overview, underscoring the city's critical position in India's history and its ongoing influence on the development of the nation's cultural and economic landscape.

Architectural Heritage

Mumbai's architectural legacy is a fascinating fusion of forms that displays a wide range of colonial, modern, and historical influences. An examination of the city's architectural wonders is provided below:

Colonial Legacy:

1. Gateway of India:

Built as a memorial to King George V and Queen Mary's 1911 landing, Mumbai's famous arch monument is a towering reminder of the city's colonial heritage. With elaborate latticework and elaborate domes, its Indo-Saracenic architectural style combines Islamic and Hindu architectural features.

2. Chhatrapati Shivaji Maharaj Terminus (CSMT):

This UNESCO World Heritage Site, formerly known as Victoria Terminus, is a masterwork of architecture. Frederick William Stevens' Gothic Revival-style station is a magnificent example of Victorian architecture, with its turrets, spires, and fine workmanship.

Historical Landmarks:
3. Taj Mahal Palace:
This historic hotel is a picture of beauty and grandeur with a touch of old-world charm. With elaborate decorations, domes, and elegant arches, its Indo-Saracenic architecture displays a fusion of Indian, Moorish, and Oriental traditions.

4. Bombay High Court:
This Gothic-style edifice, created by renowned British architect Sir Gilbert Scott, is a well-known landmark. Its remarkable columns, elaborate carvings, and spectacular façade all capture the architectural magnificence of the British colonial era.

Religious Structures:
5. Chhatrapati Shivaji Maharaj Vastu Sangrahalaya (formerly Prince of Wales Museum):
This museum, which features an impressive collection of artwork, antiquities, and archeological displays, is a superb example of Indo-Saracenic architecture. Visitors are

enthralled by its grand dome, detailed carvings, and blend of Western and Indian architectural elements.

6. Haji Ali Dargah:
Situated on a small islet near Worli, this magnificent mosque and tomb exhibits Indo-Islamic architectural design. There is a causeway leading up to the building, which has exquisite marble work and a gorgeous white dome.

Modern Marvels:
7. The Bandra-Worli Sea Link:
This cable-stayed bridge, a feat of contemporary engineering, links the suburbs of Worli and Bandra. Its modern architecture and svelte form have made it an iconic representation of Mumbai's infrastructural growth.

8. Antilia:
Mukesh Ambani's mansion is among the priciest private homes in the world. He is the richest man in India. This soaring skyscraper, with its distinctive features and amenities, combines modern architectural concepts with sumptuous luxury.

Art Deco Heritage:
9. Marine Drive:

This seafront promenade, also referred to as the Queen's Necklace, features an amazing collection of Art Deco buildings. These buildings' pastel hues, geometric designs, and symmetrical lines create an eye-catching skyline.

Mumbai's architectural legacy spans a wide range of styles, with each building telling a tale of the city's progress from colonial times to the present. The city has a rich history of cultural fusion. Mumbai's architectural treasures are a voyage through time and artistic creativity, whether one is appreciating religious buildings, colonial remains, or modern marvels.

Iconic Landmarks

Mumbai's cultural, historical, and architectural significance is embodied in several renowned sites that dot the city. A few of the city's most recognizable landmarks are shown here:

1. Gateway of India:
With pride, this magnificent arch monument faces the Arabian Sea.

Constructed to honor King George V and Queen Mary's 1911 visit, it stands as a famous emblem of Mumbai. It is a must-see landmark because of its beautiful setting, elaborate carvings, and Indo-Saracenic architectural style.

2. Chhatrapati Shivaji Maharaj Terminus (CSMT):

This UNESCO World Heritage Site, formerly known as Victoria Terminus, is a busy railway station that serves as a reminder of Mumbai's colonial-era architecture. Both commuters and tourists are enthralled with its elaborate details, turrets, pointed arches, and Gothic Revival architecture.

3. Palace of Taj Mahal:

An architectural marvel, the Taj Mahal Palace Hotel is the pinnacle of elegance and luxury. This old hotel, which dates back to 1903, combines Indo-Saracenic, Neo-Gothic, and Moorish styles. It features beautiful domes, exquisite embellishments, and a long history.

4. Marine Drive:

Marine Drive is a charming promenade that winds around the Arabian Sea. It is often referred to as the "Queen's Necklace" because of its dazzling lights at night. This boulevard's Art Deco-style buildings provide tranquil surroundings and stunning vistas.

5. Haji Ali Dargah:
Accessible via a causeway, this magnificent mosque and tomb complex is situated on a small islet off the coast of Worli. Pilgrims and tourists seeking spirituality and beautiful architecture are drawn to it by its Indo-Islamic architecture, which features a white marble dome and elaborate designs.

6. Elephanta Caves:
Located on Elephanta Island, near Mumbai's shore, these ancient rock-cut caverns date back to the 5th and 8th centuries and are recognized as a UNESCO World Heritage Site. One of the most impressive sculptures in the caves is the enormous Trimurti figure, which represents Lord Shiva's three faces.

7. Hanging Gardens (Pherozeshah Mehta Gardens):
These terraced gardens, perched atop Malabar Hill, provide expansive views of the Arabian Sea and the metropolitan

skyline. Decorated with paths, vibrant flowers, and topiary, it offers a tranquil haven in the middle of Mumbai's busy streets.

8. Siddhivinayak Temple:

Siddhivinayak is a well-known Hindu temple devoted to Lord Ganesha that draws worshippers from all over. The temple is a prominent religious landmark in Mumbai because of its architecture and meditative atmosphere.

9. Bandra-Worli Sea Link:

Offering a smooth drive and expansive views of the Arabian Sea, this renowned cable-stayed bridge links the communities of Bandra and Worli. Its remarkable engineering and architectural design have elevated it to the status of an icon of Mumbai's contemporary infrastructure.

10. Film City:

Bollywood, the Hindi film industry of India, is centered in Mumbai's Film City, which is situated in Goregaon. Even though it's closed to the public, its existence represents Mumbai's impact on the Indian entertainment industry.

Together, these well-known sites tell the tale of Mumbai's rich cultural diversity, architectural brilliance, religious significance, and varied history. They also encourage tourists to discover and take in Mumbai's many facets.

Chapter 2: Navigating Mumbai's Neighborhoods

Exploring South Mumbai

A fascinating trip through history, culture, and architectural wonders is South Mumbai exploration. This is a list of some of the noteworthy sights in this energetic area of the city:

1. Gateway of India:
Start your investigation at this famous landmark. Take in the majesty of the arch that overlooks the Arabian Sea and observe the flurry of activity that surrounds one of Mumbai's most well-known sites.

2. Chhatrapati Shivaji Maharaj Vastu Sangrahalaya (formerly Prince of Wales Museum):
Visit this museum to immerse yourself in history and art. Explore a comprehensive collection of art, sculptures, and antiques

spanning millennia, and see its remarkable Indo-Saracenic architecture.

3. Kala Ghoda Art Precinct:
Wander around this energetic art quarter, which is well-known for its street art, museums, and galleries. The Kala Ghoda Arts Festival, which features a variety of artistic, musical, and cultural expressions, brings the neighborhood to life.

4. Colaba Causeway:
Enjoy a shopping extravaganza at this lively street market. It's a shoppers' paradise, with everything from fashion boutiques to antique stores and street vendors offering anything from handicrafts to clothing.

5. Colaba and Fort Area:
Explore the quaint cafes, colonial architecture, and historic buildings that dot the neighborhoods of Colaba and Fort. Investigate avenues such as Horniman Circle, Kala Ghoda, and the Fort History precinct.

6. Elephanta Caves (via Ferry from Gateway of India):
Discover the historic rock-cut caves on Elephanta Island by taking a ferry ride there. Admire the magnificent artwork and

sculptures, particularly the well-known Trimurti statue honoring Lord Shiva.

7. Palace of Taj Mahal:
Appreciate the magnificence of this old hotel, a marvel of Indo-Saracenic design. Give it some time to sink in and enjoy its exquisite design, minute details, and deep history.

8. Marine Drive:
Take a stroll along Marine Drive, popularly known as the Queen's Necklace, to cap off your day. Savor the tranquil atmosphere, breathtaking sunset views, and the charming row of Art Deco buildings bordering the waterfront.

9. Haji Ali Dargah:
A causeway leads to this respected mosque and tomb complex, which is slightly outside of the immediate South Mumbai neighborhood yet offers a unique blend of spirituality and architectural beauty.

10. Crawford Market and Victoria Terminus (Chhatrapati Shivaji Maharaj Terminus):
If you have time, visit Crawford Market, a busy marketplace with a wide selection of products. Admire the Chhatrapati Shivaji

Maharaj Terminus' magnificent architecture as well. It is a UNESCO World Heritage Site.

Discovering South Mumbai takes you on an enthralling tour through fascinating historical sites, colorful markets, and architectural wonders. It offers a chance to experience the spirit of this vibrant city and a peek into its rich history.

Venturing through Central Mumbai

Discovering Central Mumbai provides a fusion of contemporary architecture, cultural attractions, and historical sites. This is a guide to help you see some of the noteworthy sights in this energetic area of the city:

1. Dadar Flower Market:

Start your day in one of the busy markets in Mumbai. The Dadar Flower Market is a great place for photographers and people looking for a genuine local experience because of its vivid assortment of flowers, which creates a beautiful sight.

2. Siddhivinayak Temple:
Visit this hallowed Hindu temple honoring Lord Ganesha. Take in the atmosphere of spirituality and religious zeal as worshippers honor the Lord.

3. Mahalaxmi Dhobi Ghat:
See the biggest outdoor laundry in the world. This old-fashioned outdoor laundry offers a fascinating look into Mumbai's distinctive laundry system with its rows of wash pens where Dhobis (laundrymen) handwash garments.

4. Haji Ali Dargah (Close to Worli):
A causeway leads to this famous mosque and tomb complex, which is situated just outside of Central Mumbai but offers a unique blend of spirituality and gorgeous Indo-Islamic architecture.

5. Worli Sea Face:
Take pleasure in a walk along the Worli Promenade. This calm waterfront offers expansive views of the Arabian Sea and a tranquil haven from the bustle of the city.

6. The Nehru Science Center
Visit this interactive scientific museum to learn about science and technology. Take part in interactive displays, planetarium

performances, and age-appropriate educational activities.

7. Mahalaxmi Racecourse:
Take in the grandeur of the best horse racetrack in Mumbai. The racecourse's beautiful architecture and lush landscaping are worth seeing even if you're not a fan of horse racing.

8. High Street Phoenix and Palladium Mall:
Enjoy your meals and shopping at these elegant malls. These retail centers offer upscale dining options, fashionable stores, worldwide brands, and entertainment options for an opulent experience.

9. Dr. Bhau Daji Lad Museum:
Discover the oldest museum in Mumbai, which is renowned for its artifact collection, historical exhibits, and displays honoring the cultural legacy of the city.

10. Bandra-Worli Sea Link (Viewpoint):
Even though it's a little bit out of the way, the trip is worthwhile to visit a viewpoint that provides a wide-angle view of the Bandra-Worli Sea Link. Admire the

architectural wonder that ties the suburbs together.

Exploring Central Mumbai is a rewarding way to see this unique area of the city because it offers a variety of activities such as religious tours, strolls by the sea, and insights into the modern lifestyle of the city.

Embracing Suburban Mumbai

Discovering Mumbai's suburban areas provides a variety of quiet parks, quiet streets, and cultural events. This is a guide to help you see some of the most noteworthy sights in this large area of the city:

1. Bandra:
Bandra-Worli Sea Link Viewpoint: you may get breathtaking vistas of the famous bridge that links Worli and Bandra.
Bandra Fort: This old fort offers expansive views of the Worli Sea Link and the Arabian Sea.
2. Juhu Beach:

This well-liked beach location is a great place to unwind. Savor the lively environment, regional street cuisine, and tranquil sunsets beside the Arabian Sea.

3. Powai Lake:

Get away to this gorgeous lake that is encircled by vegetation. Savor serene moments, calm walks, and boat excursions away from the bustle of the city.

4. Versova Beach:

Discover the mellow allure of this less frequented beach. Take in the serene atmosphere by the water while observing fishermen at work.

5. Goregaon's Film City:

Bollywood's center is Film City, however it's closed to the public. One of the highlights is seeing the studios and the bustling film industry from a distance.

6. Dharavi:

Take a guided tour of the biggest slum in Asia. Learn about the thriving neighborhood, local small businesses, and people's tenacity.

7. Sanjay Gandhi National Park:

Discover this enormous urban green space. In the middle of the city, explore nature trails, see the Kanheri Caves, and discover a variety of flora and wildlife.

8. Chhota Kashmir (Aarey Colony):
Explore a calm park with scenery reminiscent of Kashmir. Savor tranquil surroundings, verdant gardens, and lakeside boat cruises.

9. Global Vipassana Pagoda (Gorai Island):
Admire this magnificent pagoda, a representation of spirituality and tranquility. Reachable via ferry, it provides tranquil surroundings and expansive vistas.

10. Carter Road Promenade:
Take in Carter Road's vibrant atmosphere. Locals love to stroll along this busy promenade, which also offers a lively nightlife.

11. Andheri Lokhandwala Market:
Enjoy eating and shopping in this vibrant market, which is well-known for its hip restaurants, street shopping, and designer retailers.

12. Elephanta Caves (Accessible via Ferry from Gateway of India):
Visiting these UNESCO-listed caves on Elephanta Island makes for an enriching

day trip from Mumbai, even though it's not exactly suburban.

A comprehensive tour of Mumbai's outer boundaries, Embracing Suburban Mumbai offers a varied tapestry of experiences, from calm lakesides and beaches to cultural interactions, green areas, and peeks into the city's entertainment sector.

Chapter 3: Cultural Encounters

Arts and Entertainment

Mumbai is home to a thriving arts and entertainment sector that provides a wide variety of cultural activities. This is a guide to some of the creative and fun things to do in the city:

1. Kala Ghoda Art Precinct:

Kala Ghoda Arts Festival: The annual Kala Ghoda Arts Festival takes place in February and offers a festival of visual arts, music, dance, and literature. Numerous galleries in the precinct display exhibitions of contemporary art and cultural events.

2. Prithvi Theatre (Juhu):

Theatrical Performances: Take in plays, musicals, and cultural events at this venerable theater. It is recognized for encouraging theater arts and organizes a wide range of events.

3. National Centre for the Performing Arts (NCPA):

Music and Dance: At this well-known cultural center, take in top-notch productions such as ballet, opera, modern dance acts, and concerts of classical music.

4. Jehangir Art Gallery:
Art Exhibitions: View paintings, sculptures, and installations created by Indian and foreign artists in both traditional and modern art shows.

5. Street Art in Bandra:
Bandra's Graffiti Art: Wander through the streets of Bandra and take in the rich street art and graffiti that reflects the artistic expression of the city.

6. Bollywood Studio Tours:
Film City: Although not fully open to the public, guided tours provide information on Bollywood film sets, production methods, and behind-the-scenes looks.

7. Live Music and Nightlife:
Mumbai's Nightclubs: Take advantage of the lively nightlife of the city by visiting a variety of bars and clubs that feature DJ sets, live music acts, and a wide spectrum of musical genres.

8. Dance and Music Classes:

Cultural Workshops: Take part in lessons and workshops that teach you how to perform traditional Indian dances like Bollywood, Kathak, and Bharatanatyam.

9. Street Performances and Markets:

Local Markets: Visit markets that frequently feature street performers presenting music, dance, and other abilities, such as Colaba Causeway, Linking Road, and others.

10. Film Screenings and Film Festivals:

Mumbai Film Festival: During this yearly celebration of global cinema, take in screenings and film-related events.

11. Comedic Clubs:

Stand-up Comedy Shows: Take in the humor of the city with stand-up comedy performances, which take place at different locations all across Mumbai.

12. Mumbai Opera House (Royal Opera House):

Cultural Performances: At this renovated historical site, take in a variety of cultural performances, such as ballets, operas, musicals, and classical concerts.

Mumbai's arts and entertainment sector offers a wide range of cultural events, from traditional performances to contemporary expressions, catering to a vast range of preferences and making sure something is interesting for every enthusiast in this energetic city.

Festivals and Celebrations

Mumbai is a city that exhibits its rich cultural legacy by welcoming festivities and celebrations with tremendous zeal. The following is a list of some of the colorful festivals and events that liven up the city:

1. Ganesh Chaturthi:

September: In honor of Lord Ganesha's arrival, this 10-day event is held. On the last day, Mumbai bursts into vibrant decorations, intricate processions, and the submersion of Ganesha idols in the Arabian Sea, all accompanied by music and dance.

2. Diwali (Festival of Lights):

October/November: Diwali lights up the city with fireworks, lights, and celebrations, signifying the victory of light over darkness.

Lamps and vibrant decorations adorn homes, streets, and marketplaces.

3. Navratri and Dandiya Raas:

October: Take part in traditional dances like Garba and Dandiya Raas to commemorate the nine nights of Navratri. Several locations throughout the city host exciting dance parties.

4. Holi

March: Take in the vivid hues of Holi, a joyous celebration of colors. Residents and guests gather to dance, play with powdered colors, and enjoy the start of spring.

5. Christmas and New Year's Eve:

December: Beautifully adorned churches, markets, and a joyful atmosphere at Christmas highlight Mumbai's cosmopolitan nature. Throughout the city, there are celebrations, fireworks, and parties on New Year's Eve.

6. Eid-ul-Fitr and Eid-ul-Adha:

Varies (Based on the Islamic Calendar): Take in the festive Eid celebrations, which include prayers, feasting, and gift-giving among Muslims.

7. Kala Ghoda Arts Festival:

February: The visual arts, music, dance, theater, and literature are all celebrated throughout this colorful nine-day festival. It takes place in the Kala Ghoda art area and includes exhibitions, workshops, performances, and installations.

8. Mount Mary Fair (Bandra Fair):

September: During this week-long festival, which draws adherents of all faiths who come to seek blessings and take part in celebrations, visit the Mount Mary Basilica in Bandra.

9. Banganga Festival:

January/February: This two-day music event features traditional Indian music and dance performances in the famous Banganga Tank in Walkeshwar Temple.

10. Mumbai International Film Festival (MIFF):

Every Two Years: Every two years celebrate cinema with international short and documentary film screenings, conversations, seminars, and filmmaker connections.

Mumbai's festivals and celebrations invite both residents and visitors to share in the city's joyful spirit by providing a rainbow of cultural experiences, customs, and colorful celebrations that showcase the city's variety and community harmony.

Local Traditions and Customs

The complex cultural fabric of Mumbai is reflected in the local traditions and customs, which amalgamate habits and practices from multiple communities. The following are some salient features of Mumbai's regional traditions and customs:

1. Ganesh Chaturthi:

Idol Immersion: The city comes alive with the installation of ornate Ganesha idols in homes and public pandals on Ganesh Chaturthi. These idols are submerged in the Arabian Sea during the 10-day festival, which is marked by processions, music, and intense revelry.

2. Street Food Culture:

Vibrant Food Scene: A key component of Mumbai's character is its street food culture. Locals love and savor the wide variety of street food options offered throughout the city, from vada pav, pav bhaji, and bhel puri to kebabs and seafood delights.

3. Dabbawalas:
Lunchbox Delivery System: Using a special and complex coding system, the city's dabbawalas who are renowned for their exceptional efficiency deliver prepared meals from homes to workplaces, maintaining a history of dependability and punctuality.

4. Multi-faith Festivals:
Celebration of Various Festivals: People of Mumbai's various faiths enthusiastically celebrate one other's holidays and engage in one another's customs and rituals, promoting a culture of harmony within the community.

5. Traditional Attire:
Blend of Modern and Traditional Dress: Although Mumbai welcomes modern fashions, traditional clothes such as kurta-pajamas, dhotis, and sarees continue to be important for religious events, weddings, and festivals.

6. Street Markets and Bazaars:

Shopping Traditions: Bargaining and haggling over pricing are common habits when shopping for various items and commodities in Mumbai's local marketplaces and bazaars, which are centers of dynamic activity.

7. Religious Practices:

Visiting Places of Worship: Locals practice their faiths and participate in religious rites and prayers at a variety of places of worship, such as churches, mosques, gurudwaras, and temples.

8. Communal Spirit:

Community Building: The neighborhoods of Mumbai frequently promote a strong sense of community. Social events, religious rites, and festivals bring the community together, fostering a sense of solidarity and belonging.

9. Hospitality and Warmth:

Welcoming Guests: Mumbai residents are renowned for their friendliness and warmth, welcoming visitors into their homes with food, chai (tea), and a cordial greeting as a sign of friendship.

10. Mumbai Local Trains:

Shared Commuting Experience: The city's local trains are a phenomenon of culture as well as a means of transportation. On their everyday commute, locals travel together, exchange experiences, and develop a special kind of friendship.

Mumbai's distinctive combination of customs that characterize the city's spirit is fostered by the city's diverse and inclusive culture, which is reflected in the local traditions and customs.

Chapter 4: Culinary Delights

Street Food Extravaganza

Mumbai is well known for its wide variety of delicious street food options, providing foodies with a culinary feast. This is a guide to the best street food in the city:

1. Vada Pav:

Where to Find: Found at several citywide street kiosks and vendors.

Description: A traditional snack from Mumbai, vada is a spicy potato fritter wrapped in a pav (bread roll) and topped with chutneys.

2. Pav Bhaji:

Where to Find: Pav Bhaji stands may be found in local markets, Chowpatty, and Juhu Beach.

Description: Pav (buttered bread rolls) and bhaji (a delicious mixture of mashed vegetables cooked in spices) are eaten together.

3. Bhel Puri:

Where to Find: Juhu Beach and Girgaum Chowpatty street vendors.

Description: A blend of crispy noodles, veggies, chutneys, and puffed rice that has a sour and spicy flavor.

4. Golgappa's Pani Puri:

Where to Find: Ghatkopar and Colaba Causeway are two popular locations for finding pani puri vendors in the city.

Described as crispy hollow puris packed with a blend of spices, tamarind chutney, potatoes, and chickpeas.

5. Dahi Puri:

Where to Find: Dadar, Andheri, and Chowpatty are good places to find chaat stalls.

Description: A wonderful explosion of flavors, these small crispy puris are packed with a variety of yogurt, chutneys, potatoes, and spices.

6. Rolls and Kebabs:

Where to Find: Street vendors in different regions along Mohammed Ali Road in Colaba.

Description: Juicy kebabs with a variety of tastes and spices are served on skewers or wrapped in roomali roti.

7. Sev Puri:

Where to Find: Vendors and chaat kiosks all around the city.

Description: A tangy and delicious snack made of crisp puris topped with diced potatoes, onions, chutneys, and sev (crunchy noodles).

8. Misal Pav

Where to Find: Dadar, Thane, and Matunga local restaurants.

Described as a spicy curry cooked with sprouted lentils (misal) and eaten with pulav, it's frequently topped with lemon, onions, and crispy farsan.

9. Dabeli:

Where to Find: Dadar and Girgaum are good places to find street vendors.

Description: A blend of sweet and spicy potatoes served in a pav, topped with peanuts, chutneys, and pomegranate seeds.

10. Falooda and Kulfi:

Where to Find: Mohammed Ali Road, Crawford Market, Juhu; local dessert stalls and kulfi walas.

Description: A delightful delicacy of creamy kulfi (Indian ice cream) and falooda (vermicelli dish), accompanied with rose syrup, almonds, and seeds.

Mumbai's street food provides a genuine taste of the city's dynamic culture and diverse culinary offerings, taking visitors on a delectable trip through a variety of salty, spicy, and sweet treats.

Regional Cuisines

Mumbai, a cultural melting pot, provides a wide variety of regional Indian cuisines. Here's a guide to some of the city's most well-known regional cuisines:

1. Maharashtrian Cuisine:

Where to Find: The city's local restaurants and eateries.

Highlights: Savor traditional Maharashtrian cuisine, like batata vada, ukadiche modak, puran poli, and vada pav.

2. Cuisine of South India:

Where to Find: Local eateries, Matunga food places, and Udipi restaurants.

Highlights: Taste the traditional South Indian thalis, rasam, sambar, vadas, and idlis.

3. Gujarati Cuisine:

Where to Find: Charni Road and Kalbadevi, as well as restaurants serving Gujarati thali.

Highlights: Savor the delicious array served in a Gujarati thali, as well as dhokla, khandvi, fafda, and thepla.

4. Punjabi and North Indian Cuisine:

Where to Find: Eateries in neighborhoods like Juhu, Andheri, and Bandra.

Highlights: Savor a range of kebabs, paneer tikka, tandoori roti, butter chicken, and dal mahani.

5. Coastal Cuisine - Malvani and Konkani:

Where to Find: Specialty seafood restaurants and coastal locations.

Highlights: Savor delectable dishes of fresh seafood such as fish curry, sol kadhi, bombil fry, and the aromatic Malvani masalas.

6. Parsi Cuisine:

Where to Find: Dadar, Fort, and Colaba are home to renowned Parsi restaurants.

Highlights: Sample the Parsi-style biryanis, salli boti, dhansak, and patra ni machi.

7. Bengali Cuisine:
Where to Find: A few restaurants and Bengali sweet stores.
Highlights: Indulge in delicacies including sandesh, roshogolla, fish curry, and Bengali-style desserts.

8. Mughlai Cuisine:
Where to Find: Mohammed Ali Road, Colaba, Bandra is home to restaurants that specialize in Mughlai cuisine.
Highlights: Savor-rich, aromatic gravies like butter chicken, nihari, biryanis, and kebabs.

9. Hyderabadi Cuisine:
Where to Find: A few eateries that serve kebabs and biryani from Hyderabad.
Highlights: Savor the delicious haleem, kebabs, mirchi ka salan, and biryani from Hyderabad.

10. Tibetan and Indo-Chinese Cuisine:
Where to Find: Selected eateries and areas around Colaba Causeway.
Highlights: Sample Indo-Chinese delicacies including spicy chicken and hakka noodles, as well as momos and thukpa.

11. Keralan Cuisine:
Where to Find: Local eateries with a focus on Kerala food and restaurants offering the cuisine.
Highlights: Sample the banana leaf dinners, Kerala-style fish curry, avial, stew, and appam.

Mumbai's varied food scene showcases India's rich culinary legacy by providing both locals and tourists with a wide variety of genuine regional flavors from throughout the nation.

Fine Dining Experiences

Mumbai offers a wide variety of exquisite eating options to suit a wide range of preferences and tastes. Here's a list of some of the most upscale restaurants in the city:

1. Wasabi by Morimoto (Taj Mahal Palace):
Cuisine: Japanese
Highlights: Distinguished by its superb sashimi and sushi, as well as its modern Japanese cuisine created by renowned chef Masaharu Morimoto.

2. Ziya (The Oberoi):

Cuisine: Contemporary Indian
Highlights: Chef Vineet Bhatia, who is a Michelin star, has curated an inventive spin on traditional Indian food.

3. The Table (Colaba):
Cuisine: Modern and International
Highlights: Distinguished by its use of seasonal and regional products, the menu features a wide range of international influences.

4. Masque (Mahalaxmi):
Cuisine: Farm-to-Table Modern Indian
Highlights: Offers a tasting menu that highlights Indian tastes with a modern touch, celebrating seasonal and local ingredients.

5. Bombay Canteen (Lower Parel):
Cuisine: Modern Indian
Highlights: Highlights local flavors and ingredients with a menu influenced by various Indian cuisines in a vibrant setting.

6. Olive Bar & Kitchen (Bandra):
Cuisine: European and Mediterranean
Highlights: Provides a varied assortment of beverages and Mediterranean-inspired meals in a sophisticated atmosphere.

7. KOKO (Lower Parel):

Cuisine: Asian and Pan-Asian

Highlights: Sushi, dim sum, and other Asian-inspired delicacies are available in this modern Asian restaurant with a chic atmosphere.

8. Trishna (Fort):

Cuisine: Seafood and coastal

Highlights: Well-known for its mouthwatering seafood meals from the shore, especially its butter garlic crab and other local favorites.

9. Bastian (Bandra):

Cuisine: Modern Seafood

Highlights: Serves a variety of seafood meals made with fresh ingredients, such as sushi and grilled fish.

10. Yauatcha (Bandra Kurla Complex):

Cuisine: Dim Sum and Cantonese

Highlights: Known for its modern Cantonese food presented in an elegant environment, tea pairings, and dim sum.

11. San-Qi (Four Seasons Hotel):

Cuisine: Pan-Asian and contemporary

Highlights: Features live cooking stations and a wide variety of Pan-Asian cuisine, including Chinese delicacies, Thai curries, and Japanese sushi.

12. The Bombay Brasserie (Worli):
Cuisine: Indian and modern brasserie
Highlights: Features a menu that combines traditional and modern ingredients, offering a modern spin on Indian cuisine.

These sophisticated eating establishments in Mumbai provide a variety of delectable dishes, creative menus, and opulent surroundings to suit the tastes of discriminating diners as well as tourists.

Chapter 5: Urban Exploration

Bustling Markets and Bazaars

Mumbai is well known for its colorful marketplaces and bazaars, each of which provides a distinctive shopping experience and an insight into the lively culture of the city. The following are a few of Mumbai's busiest marketplaces and bazaars:

1. Crawford Market:

Specialty: Household goods, spices, and fresh produce

Highlights: A lively market with colorful kiosks selling a range of home items as well as fruits, vegetables, spices, and flowers.

2. Colaba Causeway:

Specialty: Clothes, Accessory Items, Handmade Items

Highlights: Trendy apparel, jewelry, accessories, antiquities, and souvenirs are available at this vibrant street market.

renowned for its unique treasures and bargains.

3. Chor Bazaar (Thieves' Market):
Specialty: Furniture, Antiques, and Vintage Items

Highlights: An amazing collection of vintage products, furniture, antiques, and one-of-a-kind rarities, including oddball objects and antiquities.

4. Linking Road (Bandra):
Specialty: Clothes and Street Shopping

Highlights: Well-known for its street booths, stylish boutiques, and extensive selection of apparel, accessories, and shoes at various price points.

5. The Zaveri Bazaar:
Specialty: Gold, silver, and jewelry

Highlights: Known for its extensive assortment of gold, silver, diamonds, and gemstones, this market is one of the biggest jewelry markets in India.

6. Dadar Flower Market:
Specialty: Garlands and Flowers

Highlights: Especially during the holiday seasons, a vibrant assortment of fresh flowers, garlands, and floral arrangements are available at this bustling market.

7. Dharavi Leather Market:
Specialty: Purses, Wallets, and Accessory Items
Highlights: Known for their fine craftsmanship, this company offers a wide range of leather goods, such as wallets, belts, purses, and accessories.

8. Bhuleshwar Market:
Specialty: Textiles and Religious Objects
Highlights: An old-fashioned bazaar well-known for its puja supplies, textiles, religious objects, and traditional Indian apparel.

9. Hindmata Market:
Specialty: Clothes and Textiles
Highlights: Well-known for its affordable ready-made apparel, textiles, and materials offered at wholesale and retail locations.

10. Mangaldas Market (Kalbadevi):
Specialty: Dress materials and textiles
Highlights: Shops offering a broad variety of fabrics, including silks, cotton, embroidery, and dress materials, make up this fabric haven.

11. Lamington Road:
Specialty: Computer and electronic goods

Highlights: Known as the electronics hub of Mumbai, it has an abundance of stores selling gadgets, laptops, and accessories linked to IT.

12. Mutton Street (Extension of Chor Bazaar):

Specialty: Vintage Pieces and Antiques

Highlights: An expansion of Chor Bazaar that sells curios, brassware, antique furniture, and vintage décor.

Mumbai's colorful markets and bazaars provide a vast array of experiences, from shopping for jewelry and textiles to discovering antique treasures, catering to a wide spectrum of interests.

Modern Skyline and Infrastructure

Mumbai's skyline is proof of its modern architectural wonders and constantly changing infrastructure. The contemporary skyline and infrastructure of the city are highlighted by the following points:

1. Bandra-Worli Sea Link:

Description: Distinguished cable-stayed bridge that spans from Bandra to Worli, providing expansive vistas and cutting down on commuting time between the suburbs and South Mumbai.

2. BKC (Bandra Kurla Complex):
Description: Mumbai's commercial area, a powerhouse for banking and commerce, is home to slick skyscrapers, corporate offices, opulent hotels, and exposition centers.

3. Mumbai Metro:
Description: The rapid transit system helps to relieve traffic congestion by connecting different regions of the city with an increasing network of metro lines.

4. Lodha World Towers:
Description: Located in the Lower Parel neighborhood, this towering residential skyscraper in Mumbai offers opulent apartments and contemporary conveniences.

5. The Imperial Tower (Tardeo):
Description: A luxurious residential skyscraper in South Mumbai that offers opulent apartments and luxurious living areas.

6. Antilia (Residence of Mukesh Ambani):

Description: Mukesh Ambani is the owner of one of the priciest private homes in the world, featuring lavish décor and imposing architecture.

7. One Avighna Park (Lower Parel):

Description: Known for its lavish living areas and modern design, this high-rise residential tower offers panoramic views of the city.

8. The Capital (Bandra Kurla Complex):

Description: A business development that adds to the city's commercial scene by including contemporary office spaces and facilities.

9. Mumbai Airport:

Description: The contemporary terminals, infrastructure, and facilities of Chhatrapati Shivaji Maharaj International Airport serve both domestic and international travelers.

10. World One Tower (Lower Parel):

Description: Known for its height and high-end living conditions, this opulent residential skyscraper provides stunning city vistas.

11. Wadala Truck Terminal (Underground Reservoir):
Description: This creative concept, which showcases cutting-edge infrastructure solutions, turns a truck port into an underground water reservoir.

12. Ongoing Infrastructure Projects:
Description: The city of Mumbai is currently experiencing various ongoing initiatives, such as the construction of coastal roads, the expansion of metro lines, and the improvement of infrastructure to increase urban amenities and connections.

Mumbai's modern skyline and infrastructure, which balance the city's rich cultural legacy and historical significance with cutting-edge transit systems, creative urban solutions, and contemporary architecture, represent the city's constant evolution.

Green Spaces and Retreats

Mumbai, although a busy city, has several parks and green areas that offer a break from the bustle of the city. Here are a few noteworthy parks and green spaces in the city:

1. Sanjay Gandhi National Park:

Location: East Borivali

Highlights: An expansive open space that offers a variety of flora and wildlife, hiking paths, verdant forests, and the Kanheri Caves within the city.

2. Hanging Gardens (Pherozeshah Mehta Gardens):

Location: Malabar Hill

Highlights: Include a magnificent view of the Arabian Sea, hedges shaped like animals, and well-kept gardens with tiered lawns.

3. Shivaji Park:

Location: Dadar

Highlights: A large park that is well-liked for leisure activities including yoga, running, and cultural gatherings; it is also thought to be the birthplace of Indian cricket.

4. Jijamata Udyaan (Rani Baug):

Location: Byculla

Highlights: The oldest zoo in Mumbai, complete with a botanical garden, a variety of species zoo, and family-friendly entertainment facilities.

5. Priyadarshini Park:
Location: Road Nepean Sea
Highlights: This park, which is next to the Arabian Sea, has green meadows, jogging trails, and a calm atmosphere for leisure.

6. Aarey Milk Colony:
Location: East Goregaon
Highlights: A huge area of greenery with paths, picnic areas, and the Chhota Kashmir garden that is well-known for its dairy production.

7. Horniman Circle Gardens:
Location: Fort
Highlights: A beautifully kept garden that offers a tranquil haven in the middle of the city, encircled by historic structures.

8. Powai Lake:
Location: Powai
Highlights: A man-made lake encircled by vegetation that provides a serene environment for strolls, picnics, and taking in the beautiful scenery.

9. Five Gardens (Hindu Colony):
Location: Dadar

Highlights: Including five gardens, it offers jogging paths, floral arrangements, kid-friendly play places, and a tranquil atmosphere.

10. Kamala Nehru Park:
Location: Malabar Hill
Highlights: Provides a broad perspective of the city, as well as gardens, verdant areas, and family-friendly entertainment areas.

11. Maharashtra Nature Park
Location: Dharavi
Highlights: An urban paradise with walking routes, birdwatching opportunities, and environmental education initiatives built on a former landfill.

12. Ovalekar Wadi Butterfly Garden:
Location: Thane
Highlights: A tranquil haven amidst nature, guided tours of a butterfly garden, and butterfly sightings.

Mumbai's green areas and retreats offer residents and tourists alike chances for leisure, outdoor pursuits, and a reconnection with the natural world amidst the city's built environment.

Chapter 6: Day Trips and Excursions

Nearby Getaways

Mumbai provides a range of nearby destinations perfect for weekend getaways or quick travels. These are a few well-liked locations close to Mumbai:

1. Lonavala and Khandala:

Distance: About 80 kilometers away from Mumbai

Highlights: Beautiful hill stations with waterfalls, luxuriant vegetation, Tiger's Leap, Karla and Bhaja Caves, and the renowned Lonavala chikkis.

2. Alibaug:

Distance: About 95 kilometers from Mumbai (approachable by car or ferry from the Gateway of India)

Highlights: Seaside town with immaculate beaches, water activities, old forts like Kolaba Fort, and mouthwatering cuisine.

3. Matheran:

Distance: About 80 kilometers away from Mumbai

Highlights: Include walks through the surrounding countryside, toy train rides, panoramic views from Louisa Point, and a tranquil hill station renowned for its pollution-free atmosphere.

4. Mahabaleshwar:

Distance: The distance from Mumbai is roughly 260 kilometers.

Highlights: A hill station well-known for its strawberry farms, peaceful lakes, picturesque scenery, and overlooks like Arthur's Seat and Pratapgad Fort.

5. Kashid Beach:

Distance: Approximately 125 kilometers

Highlights: White sand, crystal-clear waves, water sports, and a peaceful ambiance perfect for leisure are characteristics of this picturesque beach.

6. Lavasa:

Distance: About 190 kilometers

Highlights: A planned hill city with a quaint Italian atmosphere, a lakefront promenade, adventure sports, and panoramic splendor.

7. Igatpuri:.

Distance: About 120 kilometers away from Mumbai

Highlights: Include the well-known Tringalwadi Fort, Vipassana International Academy, hiking paths, and a hill town with green surroundings.

8. Bhandardara:

Distance: Approximately 165 kilometers

Highlights: Wilson Dam, Arthur Lake, Randha Falls, and the historic Ratangad Fort are just a few of the picturesque hill station's attractions.

9. Murud - Fort Janjira:

Distance: About 150 kilometers

Highlights: This seaside town is well-known for its immaculate beaches, water sports, and the magnificent Janjira Fort.

10. Karjat:

Distance: About 60 kilometers away from Mumbai

Highlights: Offers peaceful Kondeshwar Temple, river rafting in Ulhas River, Kondana Caves, and trekking paths.

11. Durshet:

Distance: About 80 kilometers away from Mumbai

Highlights: Adventure activities, hiking paths, and a tranquil location surrounded by beautiful forests characterize this nature-focused getaway.

12. Kamshet:
Distance: About 100 kilometers
Highlights: Calm lakes, beautiful scenery, caverns like Bhairi and Bedsa, and the paragliding hub.

These close-by escapes from Mumbai offer a welcome diversion from the bustle of the metropolis, combining natural beauty, historical landmarks, adventurous pursuits, and peaceful havens.

Beach Escapes

Mumbai's closeness to the coast makes it possible to visit several stunning beaches and coastal locations. These beach getaways are accessible from Mumbai:

1. Juhu Beach:
Location: Mumbai's western suburbs
Highlights: Well-liked city beach with a vibrant vibe, delicious street cuisine, horseback riding, and gorgeous sunsets.

2. Aksa Beach:

Location: Malad, Mumbai's western suburbs

Highlights: Offering a calm atmosphere and stunning sunsets, this beach is rather isolated in comparison to neighboring beaches.

3. Versova Beach:

Location: Mumbai's western suburbs, Andheri

Highlights: A sand-shored coastal village well-known for its fishermen and its freshly caught seafood.

4. Alibaug Beach:

Location: Alibaug is reachable from Mumbai by road or ferry

Highlights: Seafood shacks, Kolaba Fort, water sports, and a picturesque beach with fine beaches.

5. Kashid Beach:

Location: About 125 kilometers away from Bombay

Highlights: Immaculate white dunes, crystal-clear waters, water sports, and a peaceful environment perfect for unwinding.

6. Murud Beach:

Location: Murud, reachable from Mumbai via road

Highlights: A calm beach perfect for relaxing and water sports, with views of the magnificent Murud - Janjira Fort.

7. Ganpatipule Beach:

Location: About 340 kilometers away from Bombay

Highlights: A stunning, less-crowded beach with a well-known Lord Ganesha temple that provides a calm, contemplative haven.

8. Diveagar Beach:

Location: 190 kilometers or so from Mumbai

Highlights: Well-kept, picturesque beach well-known for its peace, calm, and laid-back atmosphere.

9. Revdanda Beach:

Location: Raigad district, accessible from Mumbai via road

Highlights: A serene retreat with a quiet beach and historical ruins like the Revdanda Fort.

10. Bordi Beach:

Location: About 145 kilometers from Mumbai, in the Palghar district

Highlights: A tranquil beach with crystal-clear sands, quiet waves, and breathtaking scenery.

11. Arnala Beach:

Location: About 70 kilometers from Mumbai is Arnala Island.

Highlights: A peaceful beach with opportunities for camping, water activities, and a calm atmosphere.

12. Gorai Beach:

Location: Borivali, which is reachable from Mumbai by ferry

Highlights: Resorts, water sports, a calm atmosphere, and a quiet beach with fewer people.

These beach locations near Mumbai are ideal for a fast beach trip since they provide a variety of calm shorelines, water activities, picturesque views, and a respite from the bustling city.

Historical Day Trips

Mumbai and the surrounding environs have a rich history, and many places make excellent historical day trips. Here are a few noteworthy historical locations close to Mumbai:

1. Elephanta Caves:
Location: Elephanta Island is reachable from Mumbai by ferry

Highlights: A magnificent collection of Lord Shiva sculptures can be found in ancient, rock-cut caverns that are part of a UNESCO World Heritage Site.

2. Caves of Ajanta and Ellora:
Location: Aurangabad (accessible from Mumbai by train or airplane)

Highlights: Amazing rock-cut caverns with elaborate Buddhist, Hindu, and Jain sculptures and paintings are housed in UNESCO World Heritage Sites.

3. Karla and Bhaja Caves:
Location: About 60 kilometers from Mumbai, close to Lonavala

Highlights: Historically significant Buddhist rock-cut caverns with intricately carved viharas, chaityas, and stupas.

4. Kanheri Caves:
Location: Borivali near Mumbai's Sanjay Gandhi National Park

Highlights: Buddhist rock-cut caves with ancient sculptures, stupas, and prayer rooms that date to the first century BCE.

5. Vasai Fort (Bassein Fort):
Location: About 60 kilometers from Mumbai is Vasai.

Highlights: Ruins, churches, and bastions comprise this 16th-century Portuguese colonial fortress.

6. Murud-Janjira Fort:
Location: Murud is located and can be reached from Mumbai.

Highlights: An impressive 17th-century sea fort renowned for its complex architecture, impenetrable structure, and fascinating history.

7. Pratapgad Fort:
Location: About 250 kilometers from Mumbai, close to Mahabaleshwar

Highlights: The Maratha Hill Fort, is renowned for its complex construction, historical value, and breathtaking vistas.

8. Chhatrapati Shivaji Maharaj Vastu Sangrahalaya (formerly Prince of Wales Museum):
Location: Mumbai

Highlights: An extensive collection of objects, paintings, sculptures, and ornamental arts illustrating the history and culture of India are on display in this museum.

9. Sewri Fort:

Location: Mumbai's Sewri

Highlights: A lesser-known fort from the 17th century that provides insight into Mumbai's past defense systems.

10. Mani Bhavan (Gandhi Museum):

Location: Mumbai

Highlights: A museum showcasing Mahatma Gandhi's life, possessions, and achievements in the Indian liberation movement is housed in a historic edifice.

11. Madh Fort (Versova Fort):

Location: Madh Island is reachable from Mumbai

Highlights: Beautiful views and historical ruins can be seen at this Portuguese-era coastal fort.

12. Sion Fort (Sion Hillock Fort):

Location: Mumbai's Sion

Highlights: Remaining pieces of Mumbai's ancient past can be seen at this historical fort, which dates to the 17th century.

For those who enjoy learning about and exploring history, these historical day tours from Mumbai provide an insight into India's rich legacy, which spans many eras and architectural motifs.

Chapter 7: Practical Information

Transportation Guide

Mumbai's transit options are varied and effective. Here's a thorough guide:

Local Trains:

Suburban Trains: Mumbai's lifeline, linking the city and its suburbs, is the Suburban Train. separated into lines for the West, Central, and Harbor. Ideal for traveling within the city and its environs.

Metro:

Metro Rail: The city's rapid transit network is growing. Metro Line 1 (Versova-Andheri-Ghatkopar) is one of the operational lines; further lines are being built.

BEST Buses:

Brihanmumbai Electric Supply and Transport (BEST): Covers a variety of routes throughout the city and suburbs. accessible and reasonably priced form of transportation.

Taxis and Auto Rickshaws:
Taxis: You may find black and yellow cabs all across the city. can be scheduled through applications or hailed on the street.
Auto Rickshaws: are three-wheeled taxis; the fare is typically agreed upon or metered before the trip.

Local Ferries:
Ferries: Link different portions of Mumbai to adjacent coastal areas and islands. There are ferry services to Alibaug, Elephanta Island, and other coastal locations.

Car Rentals and App-based Cabs:
Car Rentals: For convenience, several automobile rental companies provide self-drive or chauffeured vehicles.
App-based Cabs: Uber and Ola are two examples of services that offer practical point-to-point transportation.

Suburban Railways (Long-Distance):
Indian Railways: From stations such as Chhatrapati Shivaji Maharaj Terminus (CST), Dadar, and Mumbai Central, long-distance trains connect to different parts of India, making Mumbai a significant railway hub.

Monorail:

Monorail: Provides access to specific eastern suburbia locations over a restricted path (Chembur to Wadala).

Tips for Transportation in Mumbai:

Peak Hours: Make your plans appropriately as there is significant traffic on local trains and roadways during these times.

Railway Passes: If you travel frequently, think about getting a local train pass, which comes in various durations.

Prefer App: To make scheduling autos, cabs, or metro journeys easier, use transportation applications.

Cashless Payment: A lot of modes of transportation, such as cards and mobile wallets, now accept cashless payments.

Safety Tips:

Beware of Crowds: Be cautious in crowded buses, trains, and stations, particularly during rush hours.

Secure Valuables: Be cautious with your possessions, especially when using crowded public transit.

Although navigating Mumbai's transportation system can be challenging at first, if you get the hang of it, it offers effective connectivity throughout the city and beyond, accommodating a range of travel needs and budgets.

Accommodation Options

Mumbai provides a large selection of lodging choices to accommodate different tastes and price ranges. The following is a list of the various lodging options in the city:

1. Luxury Hotels:

Description: Mumbai is home to several opulent hotels with first-rate features, first-rate service, and great locations.

Examples: The Taj Mahal Palace, The Oberoi, JW Marriott Mumbai Juhu, Trident Nariman Point, and St. Regis Mumbai are a few examples.

2. Business Hotels:

Description: Hotels that offer modern amenities, services designed for business purposes, and convenient locations are largely geared toward business guests.

Examples: The Hyatt Regency Mumbai, Sofitel Mumbai BKC, Hilton Mumbai

International Airport, and ITC Grand Central are a few examples.

3. Boutique Hotels:

Description: Elegant, intimate lodgings that frequently feature distinctive themes, individualized care, and meticulous attention to detail.

Examples: The Taj Lands End, The Gordon House Hotel, The Leela Residences, and Abode Bombay are a few examples.

4. Budget and Mid-Range Hotels:

Description: A large selection of reasonably priced choices featuring cozy lodging, standard facilities, and handy locations.

Examples: Include the Hotel Bawa Continental, Hotel Suba International, ibis Mumbai Airport, and Ginger Hotels.

5. Service Apartments:

Description: Fully equipped apartments with hotel-quality amenities that are ideal for both short- and long-term stays are offered.

Examples: Ascot Neo, Lalco Residency, Tranquil Homes, and Seven Serviced Apartments are a few examples.

6. Hostels and Guesthouses:
Description: Low-cost solutions for tourists and backpackers looking for shared or private rooms with basic amenities.
Examples: Anjali Home, Horn Ok Please Hostel, Bombay Backpackers, and Backpacker Panda are a few examples.

7. Vacation Rentals and Homestays:
Description: Genuine lodging private homes, flats, or rooms provided by locals as well as the opportunity to mingle with locals.
Platforms: Homestay.com, Airbnb, and Vrbo provide a range of choices in Mumbai.

8. Resorts:
Description: Situated in the neighboring or outlying districts, these luxurious resorts provide leisure, entertainment, and beautiful scenery.
Examples: The Dukes Retreat, Della Resorts Lonavala, Radisson Blu Resort & Spa Karjat, and The Resort Madh-Marve are a few examples.

Tips for Accommodation:
Book in Advance: Especially for busy travel periods or significant occasions.

Check Reviews: Before making a reservation, check reviews and ratings across a variety of platforms.

Location: Take into account how close your points of interest or transit hubs are.

Flexible Cancellation Policies: Because travel conditions are unpredictable, choose lodgings with flexible cancellation policies.

The choice of lodging in Mumbai is contingent upon personal inclinations, itinerary requirements, and financial limitations. To ensure that you have a comfortable stay in the city, make sure your choice is based on your needs and the reason for your visit.

Essential Tips for Travelers

Here are some vital pointers for visitors to Mumbai:

1. Weather Considerations:

Monsoon Precautions: From June to September, Mumbai receives a lot of rain during the monsoon. Always have rain gear on hand, and avoid standing water.

2. Transportation Insights:

Local Trains: For a more comfortable ride, steer clear of peak hours during local rail rush hours.

Cab Safety: For convenience and safety, use pre-paid taxis or app-based taxis.

3. Currency and Payments:

Cash Availability: Make sure you have enough cash on hand because some smaller businesses might not take credit or debit.

ATMs: Find ATMs so you can easily get cash when you need it.

4. Safety Measures:

Crowded Areas: In busy areas, exercise caution to avoid being pickpocketed and make sure your possessions are secure.

5. Dress Code and Comfort:

Clothing: Wear loose clothing and take the city's weather into account. Places of worship are places where modest clothing is valued.

Footwear: Comfy shoes are a must for seeing different sights and negotiating busy places.

6. Food and Hygiene:

Street Food: Be cautious while experimenting with street food; choose freshly made dishes from clean sellers.

Hydration: Drink plenty of water, particularly in humid conditions.

7. Local Culture and Etiquette:

Respect Cultural Norms: Pay attention to regional traditions and customs, particularly in places of worship.

Greetings: 'Namaste' is a polite and customary way to greet locals.

8. Communication Tips:

Language: Basic Marathi phrases could be useful, as well as the widely spoken languages Hindi and English.

Navigation: For convenience of travel, carry a map or utilize a navigation app.

9. Emergency Contacts:

Emergency Numbers: If needed, have the phone numbers for the local police, hospitals, and embassies on hand.

10. Accommodation and Booking:

Advance Booking: Make reservations in advance for lodging, particularly during busy times of the year or for important occasions.

Check Reviews: Before deciding on a tour or lodgings, read reviews and ratings.

11. Flexibility and Patience:

Traffic Delays: Allow extra time for your trip; anticipate gridlock in several places.

Queue etiquette: Be patient, especially at busy tourist destinations.

12. Local Experiences:

Explore Local Culture: For a true feeling of Mumbai, take part in local events, and festivals, and try regional cuisine.

Embrace the Vibrancy:

When you visit Mumbai, make sure to take advantage of its vibrant atmosphere, welcoming residents, and distinctive features.

Recall that a well-prepared traveler has a more seamless and pleasurable journey. Have fun while you explore Mumbai, a bustling metropolis.

Chapter 8: Insider's Recommendations

Offbeat Experiences

Mumbai has a lot to offer in terms of unusual and distinctive experiences besides the standard tourist traps. Here are a few unusual experiences to think about:

1. Dharavi Slum Tours:

Description: Guided tours that highlight community life, companies, and activities while providing an interesting glimpse into Dharavi, the largest slum in Asia.

Highlights: Gain knowledge of neighborhood projects, cottage enterprises, and local entrepreneurship.

2. Mumbai Midnight Cycling Tours:

Description: During the slower hours of the night, organized cycling tours explore the city's streets and famous monuments.

Highlights: Take in the vibrant nightlife, well-lit streets, and recognizable monuments with little traffic in Mumbai.

3. Art Galleries and Street Art Tours:

Description: Discover Mumbai's thriving art scene by going on graffiti tours, art walks, and art galleries.

Highlights: Meet local artists, explore modern art locations, and find hidden gems in street art.

4. Parsi Food Trails:

Description: Take part in culinary excursions to learn about Parsi food, including tastings of regional specialties and visits to real Parsi restaurants.

Highlights: Taste special flavors, discover Parsi culture, and indulge in dishes like Patra ni Machhi, Sali Boti, and Dhansak.

5. Heritage Walks in South Mumbai:

Description: Heritage walks led by guides that showcase South Mumbai's hidden gems, old buildings, and colonial-era architecture.

Highlights: Learn about the lesser-known tales and background of famous buildings like Flora Fountain, Kala Ghoda, and Bombay High Court.

6. Bollywood Studio Tours:

Description: Explore movie studios to get an intimate look into Bollywood, the thriving Indian film business.

Highlights: See movie sets, learn about the process of making movies, and possibly attend a live shoot.

7. Khotachiwadi Heritage Walk:

Description: Explore Girgaon's Khotachiwadi, a historic village that features Portuguese-style homes and a vibrant local community.

Highlights: Take in the village's distinct architectural appeal, stroll through charming alleyways, and converse with people.

8. Sewri Flamingo Point:

Description: See a variety of birds and migratory flamingos in the winter months by visiting the Sewri mudflats.

Highlights: For those who love the outdoors, birdwatching is a must-do experience, especially while witnessing thousands of flamingos.

9. Banganga Tank and Walks:

Description: Discover the historic Banganga Tank in Walkeshwar, a calm haven amid the bustle of the city.

Highlights: Include exploring the ancient tank, seeing temples, and taking part in evening aarti (prayer) rituals.

10. Chor Bazaar Shopping and Antiques Hunt:

Description: Explore the well-known "Thieves' Market" to find unusual rarities, vintage items, and antiques.

Highlights: Explore the market for hidden gems, haggle for unusual items, and take in the lively atmosphere.

11. Yoga and Wellness Retreats:

Description: Participate in health programs or yoga retreats that are being provided in calm areas of Mumbai.

Highlights: Indulge in holistic wellness activities, yoga, meditation, and spa treatments to rejuvenate.

12. Kala Ghoda Arts Festival (Seasonal):

Description: See the yearly Kala Ghoda Arts Festival, which features performances, workshops, art installations, and cultural events.

Highlights: Take part in live music, literary events, various art forms, and gourmet adventures.

Beyond the typical tourist sites, these unique experiences in Mumbai provide visitors with a fresh viewpoint and let them explore the city's rich history, culture, and diverse offerings in greater detail.

Hidden Gems and Local Favorites

Mumbai is home to many undiscovered treasures and neighborhood favorites that locals and tourists seek out unusual experiences. Here are a few less well-known but lovely locations:

1. Worli Sea Face Promenade:

Description: A more sedate promenade with breathtaking views of the Bandra-Worli Sea Link and the Arabian Sea.

Highlights: Ideal for strolling in the evening, taking in sunsets, and observing the waves' rhythm.

2. Global Vipassana Pagoda:

Description: Described as the world's largest stone dome without pillars, this majestic pagoda is located in Gorai.

Highlights: The lessons of Vipassana meditation, the serene atmosphere, and the meditation hall.

3. Manori Island

Description: A short ferry ride from Marve Beach brings you to this peaceful island close to Malad.

Highlights: Genuine regional seafood, tranquil beaches, and a relaxed atmosphere.

4. Chhota Kashmir:

Description: Boating in a tiny lake and a lovely backdrop make this charming park in Goregaon famous.

Highlights: Paddle boating facilities, verdant surroundings, and a tranquil atmosphere.

5. Banganga Tank and Walkeshwar Temple:

Description: This historic water tank in Walkeshwar is encircled by temples.

Highlights: A serene environment, a spiritual atmosphere, and centuries-old buildings.

6. Haji Ali Dargah at Night:

Description: See the famous Haji Ali Dargah lit up by lights after dusk and take in its tranquil beauty.

Highlights: A serene atmosphere, breathtaking sea vistas, and a spiritual vibe.

7. Dr. Bhau Daji Lad Museum (formerly Victoria and Albert Museum):

Description: Showcasing historical relics and exhibitions, Mumbai's oldest museum is located in Byculla.

Highlights: Include the fascinating exhibits, the renovated historic structure, and the lively workshops.

8. Dadar Flower Market:

Description: Vibrant flowers and garlands are sold in this bustling Dadar market.

Highlights: A vibrant array of hues, aromatic flowers, and an energetic environment, particularly during festivals.

9. Ajoba Hill Fort Trek:

Description: This lesser-known trekking route in Shahapur leads to the Ajoba Hill Fort and is a picturesque walk.

Highlights: Stunning views from the summit, abundant biodiversity, and serene settings.

10. Mahakali Caves:

Description: Remarkable old Buddhist caverns in Andheri are sometimes disregarded in favor of other cave systems.

Highlights: Peace, historical significance, and intricately carved rock carvings.

11. Bandra Bandstand and Castella de Aguada (Bandra Fort):

Description: With a view of the Arabian Sea, there is a picturesque promenade and the remnants of an ancient fort.

Highlights: Calm strolls, stunning views of the sea, and ruins of the past.

12. Chinchpokli Cha Chintamani Ganesh Mandal:

Description: Known for its distinctive decorations and lively celebrations, this lesser-known Ganesh Mandal takes place around Ganesh Chaturthi.

Highlights: Detailed idol decorations, regional celebrations, and a customary, less congested environment.

Travelers can learn about Mumbai's lesser-known sides by investigating these hidden treasures and neighborhood favorites, which provide genuine experiences that locals and adventure seekers love.

Insider Tips for Exploring Mumbai

Here are a few insider suggestions to improve your Mumbai exploration:

1. Early Bird Advantage:

Beat the Crowds: To make the most of your time and avoid crowds, visit well-known locations early in the morning.

2. Local Culinary Delights:

Street Food Savvy: For a genuine yet secure experience, check out the neighborhood street food vendors, but remember to wash your hands frequently.

3. Navigation Hacks:

Local Insights: Mumbai residents are generally amiable and eager to assist, so don't be afraid to ask for advice or directions.

Apps for Assistance: For precise directions and up-to-date traffic information, use navigation applications.

4. Diverse Transport Experiences:

Local Train Travel: For a genuine commuter experience, take a trip on the Mumbai local train during off-peak hours.

Ferry Commute: If you're looking for a different way to get to neighboring islands like Elephanta or Alibaug, think about taking ferries.

5. Festival Participation:
Festive Vibes: For a fully immersed cultural experience, join in local celebrations during holidays like Ganesh Chaturthi or Diwali if your visit falls around those times.

6. Bargain and Negotiate:
Street Shopping: Learn how to haggle to get the greatest prices on apparel, accessories, and mementos at neighborhood markets and street sellers.

7. Photography Opportunities:
Golden Hours: Take beautiful pictures in famous spots like Marine Drive or Bandstand to capture the allure of the city at dawn or dusk.

8. Hidden Historical Gems:
Offbeat Explorations: For a fresh viewpoint, explore the city's little-known historical landmarks and forts, caves, and heritage buildings.

9. Weather Preparation:

Monsoon Readiness: Bring rain gear and waterproof bags in case of Mumbai's monsoon; throughout the rainy season, be ready for unexpected downpours.

10. Safety and Caution:

Valuables Safekeeping: Make sure everything is locked up, especially when using public transportation or in crowded areas. Be on the lookout for pickpockets.

11. Language and Communication:

Local Lingo: A few simple Marathi words or phrases can go a long way toward surprising locals and improving communication.

12. Relish the Local Vibe:

Blend In: Savor the lively energy that Mumbai has to offer and embrace the city's fast-paced lifestyle and unique culture.

You can make the most of your trip to Mumbai and take advantage of its rich culture, varied experiences, and hidden gems by paying attention to these insider suggestions.

Chapter 9: Responsible Tourism

Sustainable Travel Practices

It is imperative to adopt sustainable travel habits to mitigate environmental damage and foster conscientious tourism. Here are some eco-friendly travel recommendations for discovering Mumbai:

1. Public Transportation:

Opt for Public Transit: To cut carbon emissions and help the city's public transportation system, take advantage of local trains, buses, and metros.

2. Walking and Cycling:

Explore on Foot: Take a stroll to learn about the neighborhoods you pass through; it helps the environment and lets you experience the local way of life.

Rent Bicycles: Hiring bicycles for short trips encourages environmentally friendly transportation and offers an alternative viewpoint of the city.

3. Choose Eco-friendly Accommodations:

Eco-friendly Stays: Choose lodgings that use sustainable methods such as recycling waste, conserving water, and employing renewable energy.

4. Reduce Plastic Usage:

Carry Reusable Items: To reduce the amount of single-use plastic that you consume, bring reusable bags, utensils, and water bottles.

Refill Stations: To avoid purchasing bottled water, look for locations that offer water refill stations.

5. Responsible Sightseeing:

Respect Local Heritage: To maintain the integrity of heritage sites and natural reserves, abide by the rules.

Leave No Trace: Don't litter, and carry your trash with you until you locate suitable trash cans.

6. Support Local Businesses:

Shop Local: To support your community's economy, buy trinkets or goods from nearby producers and merchants.

Dine Locally: To support local farmers and lessen your carbon footprint, choose restaurants that serve food that is obtained locally.

7. Energy Conservation:

Conserve Energy: Even at hotels or other lodging establishments, turn off the lights, air conditioning, and devices when not in use.

Conserve Water: Pay attention to how much water you use, particularly when taking showers and brushing your teeth.

8. Eco-friendly Tours and Activities:

Choose Sustainable Tours: Go for environmentally conscious excursions that prioritize protecting the environment and conserving wildlife.

Wildlife Interaction: Encourage moral animal interactions and abstain from actions that injure or exploit wildlife.

9. Engage in Environmental Initiatives:

Participate in Clean-ups: To improve the local environment, take part in beach or community clean-up initiatives.

Learn and Educate: Get involved in local sustainability projects and educate yourself on Mumbai's environmental initiatives.

10. Spread Awareness:

Share Your Experience: Encourage people to adopt eco-friendly travel habits when they visit Mumbai or other destinations by sharing with them your sustainable travel experiences.

You may minimize your environmental effects when traveling to Mumbai in a responsible and fulfilling manner by implementing these sustainable travel habits.

Supporting Local Communities

Traveling to positively impact the locations you visit can be achieved through supporting local communities. While you're in Mumbai, consider the following ways you may help the local community:

1. Shopping and Souvenirs:

Local Markets: Shop at marketplaces like Chor Bazaar, Crawford Market, and Colaba

Causeway for textiles, artwork, and handicrafts.

Support Artisans: To help preserve traditional arts and crafts, support local artists and craftsmen by making direct purchases from them.

2. Dining and Culinary Experiences:

Eat Locally: To support your community's farmers and producers, patronize eateries and food stands that serve regional cuisine made with products that are sourced locally.

Explore Street Food: Savor the street food culture of Mumbai by visiting local eateries and small vendors for real, authentic meals.

3. Tours and Guides:

Hire Local Guides: Choose tours given by people who live in the area and are well-versed in the history, customs, and lesser-known areas of the city.

Community Tours: Seek out tours with a focus on the community that assists social causes or the local community.

4. Accommodations:

Stay in Homestays: To immerse yourself in the local way of life and to directly assist local families, think about booking a room in a homestay or guesthouse run by the locals.

Choose Locally Owned: To support the local economy, choose lodgings owned and operated by residents as opposed to big chains.

5. Volunteer Opportunities:

Community Projects: During your visit, look into and take part in volunteer activities or local community projects that are centered around social welfare, education, or conservation.

6. Arts and Performances:

Attend Local Performances: Take in customary dance, music, and theater pieces put on by regional artists or cultural institutions.

7. Eco-Tourism Initiatives:

Support Conservation Efforts: Take part in eco-tours or activities that support the preservation of the local environment, the protection of wildlife, or sustainable practices.

8. Responsible Interactions:

Respect Local Traditions: When engaging with members of the community, show consideration for their customs, traditions, and manners.

Learn and Share: Gain knowledge of regional problems, achievements, and difficulties. Then, share your own experiences to help others understand the needs of the community.

9. Feedback and Reviews:

Positive Reviews: To encourage others to support small businesses, lodgings, or experiences, and leave good reviews or feedback.

10. Engage and Learn:

Engage in Conversations: Talk to locals to learn about their lives, struggles, and stories. This will promote cross-cultural understanding and interaction.

You may positively influence the locations you visit by actively supporting local communities, which helps with their overall well-being, cultural preservation, and economic progress.

Responsible Tourism Initiatives

Initiatives aimed at promoting responsible tourism are essential for maintaining cultural traditions, encouraging sustainability, and reducing the detrimental effects of travel on places. Here are a few efforts in Mumbai promoting ethical travel and ways you may help:

1. Waste Management and Recycling:

Waste Reduction: Take part in waste reduction initiatives by properly disposing of trash and, when feasible, separating recyclables.

Support Recycling: Encourage recycling by taking part in community-driven programs that emphasize recycling and waste management, such as beach clean-ups.

2. Sustainable Accommodations:

Eco-friendly Stays: Select lodgings that adhere to eco-friendly principles such as waste minimization, water conservation, and energy efficiency.

Certified Properties: Seek out accommodations or hotels that have received certification from sustainability or eco-friendly organizations.

3. Community Tourism:

Homestays and Community Stays: To directly assist the community, choose to travel in a homestay or guesthouse run by local families.

Community Engagement: Engage with the community by taking part in workshops, local events, and cultural exchanges that help communities achieve their goals.

4. Conservation and Wildlife Preservation:

Responsible Wildlife Tours: Ethical and Responsible Wildlife Tours: Choose tours that put animal welfare first to support conservation efforts for wildlife.

Avoid Animal Exploitation: Don't encourage pursuits such as riding elephants or going to places where animals are kept in captivity.

5. Cultural Preservation:

Respect Local Culture: Respect regional traditions, customs, and places of worship; familiarize oneself with cultural standards to prevent inadvertent offense.

Support Cultural Initiatives: Encourage cultural initiatives by supporting traditional arts and crafts, going to cultural events, and purchasing goods directly from craftspeople.

6. Sustainable Transportation:

Public Transit Usage: To lessen your carbon footprint, use eco-friendly modes of transportation like walking, cycling, or carpooling.

Promote Green Transport: Back programs that advocate for the use of electric cars, bike lanes, and enhanced public transportation.

7. Water Conservation:

Conserve Water: Report leaks or waste and use caution when using water in lodgings and on excursions.

Support Clean Water Projects: Participate in or donate to regional campaigns and clean water efforts to support clean water projects.

8. Responsible Tour Operators:

Choose Ethical Operators: Choose tour companies or guides who are dedicated to sustainable tourism, community involvement, and responsible tourist practices.

9. Education and Awareness:

Share Knowledge: Encourage other travelers to reduce their influence on the environment and local communities by educating them about responsible travel practices.

Promote Sustainability: Use social media to motivate others by sharing your positive travel experiences and tales of ethical travel.

10. Support Local NGOs and Initiatives:

Volunteer Opportunities: Participate in volunteer programs that help Mumbai's community-based, social, and environmental projects.

Donate or Volunteer: Assist regional non-governmental organizations that promote community welfare, conservation, and sustainable development.

Travelers can actively support the preservation of regional cultures, the environment, and the socioeconomic well-being of the Mumbai communities they visit by taking part in responsible tourism projects.

Chapter 10: Conclusion

Farewell to Mumbai

As you bid farewell to Mumbai, here's a heartfelt parting message:

Farewell, Mumbai – City of Dreams and Diverse Wonders

Your stay has been a colorful tapestry of adventures that include ethical tourism, enjoying delicious food, discovering historical wonders, and embracing the local way of life. Take with you the memories of Mumbai's busy streets, its people's kindness, and its indomitable spirit as you depart.

I hope the city's spirit echoes follow you, bringing back memories of its rich history, the stunning skyline, and the multitude of hues that shaped your voyage. Treasure the times, the connections formed, and the knowledge acquired.

Feel the soul of Mumbai with you, whether it's the tumultuous markets, the tranquil coastline vistas, or the reverberations of aarti at historic temples. I hope and pray that your trips will be full of joy, discovery, and a dedication to responsible exploration. May your journey through life's tapestry be embellished with a variety of adventures and may the memories of Mumbai continue to be a treasured chapter until we cross paths again.

"Aamchi Mumbai, Until Next Time!"

Lasting Memories and Reflections

I hope these enduring memories help you on your next adventure as you think back on your stay in Mumbai:

Memories Painted in Mumbai's Palette:

Cultural Kaleidoscope: A Cultural Kaleidoscope Mumbai's varied customs, cheerful festivals, and hospitable people all left a lasting impression on your heart.

Iconic Landmarks: The serene Marine Drive, the ancient appeal of CST, and the imposing attraction of the Gateway of

India, which together presented a picture-perfect picture of the city.

Sensory Symphony: The enticing smells of street food in Mumbai, the chaotic rhythm of the city's local trains, and the vibrant energy that shaped its streets.

Resilient Resonance: The tales of perseverance reverberating through the busy streets, demonstrating the spirit of the city in the face of adversity.

Cultural Encounters: Having lively discussions, feeling their hospitality, and experiencing shared experiences that united people from different backgrounds and cultures.

Reflections for the Road Ahead:

Cultural Tapestry: Wherever your path takes you, pass on the appreciation of many cultures, accepting differences, and promoting understanding.

Sustainable Footprints: Allow your dedication to eco-friendly travel methods and environmental preservation to direct your upcoming adventures.

Human Connection: Treasure the relationships formed, the giggles had, and the friendships that spanned geographical borders when you were visiting Mumbai.

Resilience and Inspiration: Take a cue from Mumbai's perseverance and let it give you the fortitude to face life's obstacles head-on.

May these treasured memories and thoughts, as you say goodbye to Mumbai, act as a compass for your upcoming trips, enhancing your experiences, and adding fresh stories to the fabric of your life's experiences.

Printed in Great Britain
by Amazon